First Facts®

American Symbols

The Statue of Liberty

by Marc Tyler Nobleman

Consultant:
Melodie Andrews, Ph.D.
Associate Professor of Early American History
Minnesota State University, Mankato

Capstone press

Mankato, Minnesota

First Facts is published by Capstone Press,
1710 Roe Crest Drive, North Mankato, Minnesota 56003.
www.capstonepub.com

Library of Congress Cataloging-in-Publication Data
Nobleman, Marc Tyler.
    The Statue of Liberty / by Marc Tyler Nobleman.
    v. cm.—(First Facts. American symbols)
    Includes bibliographical references and index.
    Contents: Statue of Liberty fast facts—American symbol of freedom—A gift from
France—Bartholdi begins working—Building the Statue—Coming to America—Repairing
the Statue—Visiting the Statue—Timeline—Hands On: How Big is Lady Liberty.
    ISBN-13: 978-0-7368-1632-8 (hardcover)   ISBN-10: 0-7368-1632-1 (hardcover)
    ISBN-13: 978-0-7368-4703-2 (softcover pbk.)   ISBN-10: 0-7368-4703-0 (softcover pbk.)
    1. Statue of Liberty (New York, N.Y.)—Juvenile literature. 2. New York (N.Y.)—
Buildings, structures, etc.—Juvenile literature. [1. Statue of Liberty (New York, N.Y.)
2. Statues. 3. National monuments.] I. Title. II. American symbols (Mankato, Minn.)
F128.64.L6 N63 2003
974.7'1—dc21   2002010713

Summary: Discusses the history of the Statue of Liberty, its designer, its construction, its
    location, and its importance as a symbol of the United States.

Editorial Credits
Chris Harbo and Roberta Schmidt, editors; Eric Kudalis, product planning editor;
    Linda Clavel, cover and interior designer; Alta Schaffer, photo researcher

Photo Credits
Corbis/Bettmann, 7, 19; Robert Maass, 16
Hulton Archive by Getty Images, 9, 15
Library of Congress, 11, 12, 17, 20
Museum of the City of New York, a gift of Mrs. James P. Silo, 10
New York Public Library, 13
Photo Network/Grace Davis, 5
PhotoDisc, cover, 21
Visuals Unlimlited/C. P. George, 18

Printed in the United States of America in North Mankato, Minnesota.
062014   008258R

Table of Contents

Statue of Liberty Fast Facts

- The Statue of Liberty was a gift from France to the United States.

- French sculptor Frédéric Auguste Bartholdi designed the Statue of Liberty.

- Gustave Eiffel was a French builder who planned the iron framework inside the statue. Later, he created the Eiffel Tower in Paris, France.

- In 1884, Frédéric Auguste Bartholdi finished the Statue of Liberty in Paris, France. The statue was put together in New York Harbor in 1886.

- Some people call the statue "Lady Liberty." The official name of the Statue of Liberty is "Liberty Enlightening the World."

- In 1986, the Statue of Liberty was repaired and cleaned for its 100th birthday.

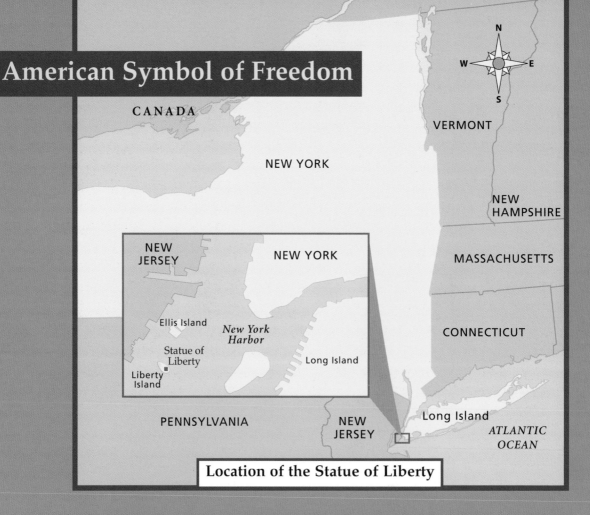

American Symbol of Freedom

CANADA

VERMONT

NEW YORK

NEW HAMPSHIRE

MASSACHUSETTS

NEW JERSEY

NEW YORK

Ellis Island

New York Harbor

Statue of Liberty

Long Island

CONNECTICUT

Liberty Island

PENNSYLVANIA

NEW JERSEY

Long Island

ATLANTIC OCEAN

Location of the Statue of Liberty

The Statue of Liberty is a symbol of freedom. It stands on Liberty Island in New York Harbor. For many years, immigrants traveled to America by boat.

The boats passed the statue in the harbor.
The Statue of Liberty made people feel
welcome in the United States.

A Gift from France

France gave the Statue of Liberty to the United States. It was a gift of friendship. Both France and the United States were free countries. The statue was a symbol of their freedom. French sculptor Frédéric Auguste Bartholdi designed the statue.

sculptor
a person who creates art by carving stone, wood, or other materials

9

Bartholdi Begins Working

In 1871, Bartholdi visited New York. He chose a place for the statue in New York Harbor. He also drew pictures of the statue. Bartholdi then returned to France to make small models of the statue. He used his mother as a model for the statue's face.

In 1875, workers began building the Statue of Liberty in Paris, France. Workers shaped large copper plates to cover the statue. The right arm and the torch were finished first.

The head was finished next. People could
visit the torch and the head. In 1884, the
statue was completed and ready to be sent
to the United States.

Coming to America

The Statue of Liberty was too big to send in one piece. Workers took it apart and shipped it in 214 crates. At the same time, Americans were building a large base for the statue. The statue and its pedestal were finished in October 1886.

pedestal
the bottom support of a statue

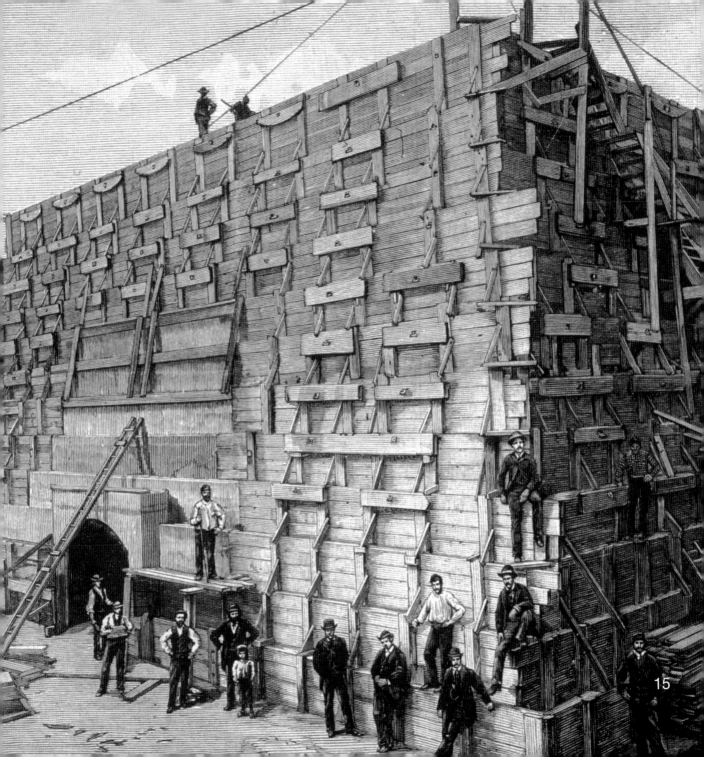

15

Repairing the Statue

Over many years, weather and pollution damaged the Statue of Liberty. In the 1980s, the statue was repaired. The torch was replaced. The copper plates were cleaned. Steel bars were added inside the statue for strength. The repairs were finished in 1986.

pollution
materials that are harmful to the environment

17

Visiting the Statue

Millions of people visit the Statue of Liberty each year. A museum in its base shows the statue's history. People can see the statue's first torch in the museum.

Visitors also can go inside the Statue of Liberty. They can climb 354 steps to the crown at the top of the statue. Visitors are reminded that the Statue of Liberty is a symbol of freedom.

Timeline

1871—Frédéric Auguste Bartholdi picks a site in New York Harbor for the statue.

1884—The French finish the statue.

1875—The French begin building the Statue of Liberty.

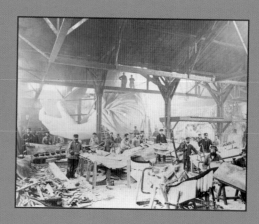

1886—The Statue of Liberty is put together on its pedestal.

1984—Workers begin to repair the statue.

1886—The Statue of Liberty opens for visitors.

1986—The Statue of Liberty is 100 years old.

Hands On: How Big is Lady Liberty?

The Statue of Liberty is 305 feet, 1 inch (93 meters) tall from the ground to the tip of the torch. You can see the size of some parts of the statue by using yarn.

What You Need

Tape Measure
Yarn
Scissors
A friend

What You Do

1. Use a tape measure to measure three pieces of yarn. Cut one piece of yarn 4 feet, 6 inches (140 centimeters) long. Cut one piece 8 feet (240 centimeters) long. Cut one piece 16 feet, 5 inches (5 meters) long.
2. Pick up the shortest piece of yarn. Pull the yarn tight between you and your friend. This piece of yarn is the same length as the Statue of Liberty's nose.
3. Pick up the medium length piece of yarn. Pull the yarn tight between you and your friend. This piece of yarn is the same length as the Statue of Liberty's index finger.
4. Now pick up the longest piece of yarn. Pull this yarn tight. This piece of yarn is the same length as the Statue of Liberty's hand.

Words to Know

design (di-ZINE)—to make a plan for how to build something

freedom (FREE-duhm)—the right to live the way you want

immigrant (IM-uh-gruhnt)—a person who leaves one country to live in another country

liberty (LIB-ur-tee)—freedom

museum (myoo-ZEE-uhm)—a place where visitors can see historical objects

pollution (puh-LOO-shuhn)—materials that are harmful to the environment

sculptor (SKUHLP-ter)—a person who creates art by carving stone, wood, or other materials

symbol (SIM-buhl)—an object that stands for something else

Read More

Rau, Dana Meachen. *The Statue of Liberty.* Let's See. Minneapolis: Compass Point Books, 2002.

Wilson, Jon. *The Statue of Liberty: A Beacon for Freedom.* Chanhassen, Minn.: Child's World, 1999.

Internet Sites

Track down many sites about the Statue of Liberty.

Visit the FACT HOUND at
http://www.facthound.com

IT IS EASY! IT IS FUN!

1) Go to *http://www.facthound.com*
2) Type in: 0736816321
3) Click on "FETCH IT" and FACT HOUND will find several links hand-picked by our editors.

Relax and let our pal FACT HOUND do the research for you!

Index